The Library Book

Illustrated by **Bill Slavin**

Maureen Sawa

The Library Book

The Story of Libraries from Camels to Computers

TUNDRA BOOKS

Published in Canada by Tundra Books,
481 University Avenue, Toronto, Ontario M5G 2E9

Published in the United States by Tundra Books of Northern New York,
P.O. Box 1030, Plattsburgh, New York 12901

Library of Congress Control Number: 2004195108

Library and Archives Canada Cataloguing in Publication

Sawa, Maureen

     The library book : the story of libraries from camels to computers /
Maureen Sawa ; Bill Slavin, illustrator.

Includes bibliographical references and index.

ISBN-13: 978-0-88776-698-5
ISBN-10: 0-88776-698-6

     1. Libraries – Juvenile literature. 2. Libraries – History – Juvenile
literature. I. Slavin, Bill. II. Title.

Z721.S29 2006   j027   C2004-907146-7

We acknowledge the financial support of the Government of Canada
through the Book Publishing Industry Development Program (BPIDP) and
that of the Government of Ontario through the Ontario Media Development
Corporation's Ontario Book Initiative. We further acknowledge the support
of the Canada Council for the Arts and the Ontario Arts Council for our
publishing program.

ONTARIO ARTS COUNCIL
CONSEIL DES ARTS DE L'ONTARIO

Printed and bound in Canada

1 2 3 4 5 6   11 10 09 08 07 06

CONTENTS

INTRODUCTION

For more than five thousand years, people have been writing about the world around them. Whether they were pressing marks into wet clay, chiseling letters into stone, or entering keystrokes into a computer, they were creating a permanent record of their thoughts and ideas and day-to-day lives. For almost equally as long, people have also been thinking of ways to store and organize those records, making them easy for others to use and preserving them for future generations. This is how libraries were born.

At first glance, today's modern, high-tech libraries may not appear to have much in common with the loose collections of clay and stone tablets of the ancient world. But even libraries that are separated by thousands of years are connected by a common goal: to provide us with information about where we've been as we move forward into the future. Libraries link people who live today with those who came before and those who are yet to be. They are places where ideas take flight.

CHAPTER ONE

In the Beginning

To prepare his young son to be king one day, Philip II, the great ruler of ancient Macedonia, hired the philosopher Aristotle as his tutor. In the three years they spent together, Aristotle and the boy who would grow up to be Alexander the Great studied everything from mathematics to music. It was Aristotle who inspired Alexander's lifelong interest in philosophy and politics, and his belief that a sound mind was as important to a great warrior and leader as a sound body. But it was Aristotle's literature lessons that Alexander enjoyed most of all. The tales of the ancient Greek heroes had a great effect on the impressionable teenager, and he began to dream of the days when he would have his own adventures in far-off lands. He even carried a copy of the epic poem the *Iliad*, the story of the great Achilles and the Trojan War, with him for the rest of his days.

Alexander's quest for wisdom and adventure took him across the known world and helped him conquer lands from the Mediterranean Sea to India. Reading remained one of his obsessions until the day he died, from fever and exhaustion, when he was just thirty-three. So deep was his love of knowledge that his successors decided that a library should be built as a tribute to him. It would be in Egypt, in the great city that he had founded and named Alexandria, after himself.

The Library of Alexandria was not the first library of ancient times, but it was the most famous one. Egypt's rulers dedicated themselves to building up its extensive collection. They borrowed scrolls, the earliest type of books, from other important cities, like Athens, and had scribes duplicate them by hand so the Alexandrian library would have its own copies.

 Although Alexandria was in Egypt, it was primarily a center of Greek culture and learning. Most of its famous library's scrolls were written in Greek.

The Paper Route

Unlike us, ancient people did not have paper to write on. It was invented in China only about two thousand years ago. Before that, people wrote on a variety of other materials, from clay tablets and stone to leather, tree bark, and silk.

The scrolls kept in the library at Alexandria were made entirely of papyrus, a reed that once flourished along the Nile River. To make papyrus scrolls, craftsmen would cut the stems of the reed into strips and then crush them into sheets that looked something like paper. These sheets were long and flexible, and could be rolled up and tied with string.

Papyrus was quite delicate, however, and didn't always last very long, so eventually it was replaced with a more durable material called parchment. Made from the skin of calves, goats, or sheep, parchment was easier to write on but didn't roll up into scrolls very well. To improve handling, and make documents easier to store, librarians began to fold the sheets of parchment in half and sew them down the fold, creating the earliest forms of what we now think of as books.

According to legend, paper made its way out of China in the 700s, in the hands of local traders. When several Chinese papermakers were captured by Arabs near the modern-day city of Samarqand, in Uzbekistan, they were forced to pass on what was to them already an ancient art. Although Arabs, in turn, brought paper to Europe in about 1000 A.D., parchment remained the writing material of choice there for several more centuries. It wasn't until the printing press was introduced to Europe in the 1400s that paper came into wide general use.

 In addition to its library, Alexandria was also famous for its lighthouse, one of the Seven Wonders of the Ancient World. Built in about 280 B.C., the lighthouse stood in the city's harbor for fifteen hundred years, keeping ships safe from the rocks, until it was destroyed by an earthquake in the 1300s.

They even detained ships in Alexandria's harbor, searching them from bow to stern for scrolls that could be confiscated and copied. If they got their scrolls back at all, the owners often found themselves in possession of the mistake-riddled (and therefore much less valuable) copies, instead of the originals. Methods like these allowed the Egyptians to quickly build up the most important library in the ancient world. In time, the Library of Alexandria had a collection of more than four hundred thousand volumes – every single scroll then known to exist.

But the library was as famous for the scholars who used it as it was for the volumes it housed. The scientists who spent their days rolling and unrolling Alexandria's thousands of

Eureka! Eureka!

The great mathematician Archimedes was one of the many scholars who went to Alexandria to study. We remember him today for his theory of displacement, also known as Archimedes' principle.

Archimedes was asked by a Greek king named Hiero to figure out whether a wreath the king had been given was made of pure gold, as the goldsmith claimed, or of a cheaper alloy of gold and silver. He decided to mull the problem over in a public bath, and when he stepped into the water and watched it slop over the sides, he had a brainstorm. He realized that he could calculate the wreath's volume by submerging it and measuring how much water overflowed, or was displaced. He could then repeat the process with a lump of pure gold. If the goldsmith was telling the truth, the wreath and the gold nugget would displace the same amount of water; if he was lying (which it turned out he was!), the wreath would displace more water than the pure gold (because silver has less weight per volume than gold).

According to legend, Archimedes was so excited by his idea that he leapt from his bath and ran naked through the streets of his native Syracuse, on the island of Sicily, shouting "*Eureka*!" (which means "I have found it!").

Hypatia of Alexandria

Unlike today's libraries, the Library of Alexandria wasn't much of a place for children. One who did spend her days wandering its corridors, however, was Hypatia. She was the daughter of Theon, the director of the Museum of Alexandria, the building that housed the library.

Inspired by her father's dedication to the arts and sciences, Hypatia grew up to be an accomplished astronomer and mathematician, as well as an expert editor. She produced several new, simpler versions of difficult texts and also wrote books explaining complex theories so students would be better able to understand them. But many people were put off by her commitment to science and the loyalty she stirred in her students. They were suspicious of her motives and thought her activities were inappropriate for a woman. Eventually, she was attacked and murdered by a group of angry citizens who were driven to violence by what they saw as her non-Christian beliefs. Her murder marked the beginning of a great religious and political divide in Alexandria, and the start of the city's slow decline as a center of learning.

Today, we remember Hypatia as the first woman astronomer and as a person who has inspired librarians and scholars for centuries. Two lunar craters are named for her, a fitting tribute to a woman who spent her life illuminating the world for others.

scrolls advanced human knowledge in many ways, from calculating the circumference of the earth to beginning to map the human body. One man, an astronomer named Aristarchus, worked there on a theory that the sun, and not the earth, was the center of the universe. About eighteen hundred years passed before Nicolaus Copernicus proved that this theory was correct!

Of course, there were libraries throughout the ancient world, not just in Alexandria. In Babylonia, an empire centered in present-day Iraq, a king called Hammurabi founded the Borsippa Library in 1700 B.C. That library was stocked with clay and stone tablets. Its most famous holding was a collection of laws called the Code of Hammurabi. Inscribed on a large stone slab called a stela, this code, which would have been prominently displayed, showed Babylonians what laws they had to obey and what punishments they would suffer if they didn't. It covered everything from debt collection to witchcraft to false accusation. Because it was written on hard stone,

The First Library

The credit for the first library goes to the Sumerians, an ancient people who lived in a place called Mesopotamia, a region that covered the modern-day nations of Iraq, Syria, and Turkey. The Sumerians invented an early form of writing known as cuneiform, probably about five thousand years ago. They made rectangular tablets of wet clay and inscribed them with cuneiform symbols, which were wedge-shaped marks that represented words or syllables. These tablets were then baked or left to dry in the sun until they hardened.

The Sumerians began to store and organize collections of their clay tablets sometime around 2700 B.C. Once they realized that these tablets, most of which were business and legal documents, were in fact permanent records of their daily lives, they established storage areas where they could be kept for future use. Because the Sumerians were so careful to preserve these written documents, hundreds of thousands of them have survived through to this day. Scholars have been able to use these tablets to uncover a wealth of information about day-to-day life in what was the world's first civilization.

instead of flimsy papyrus, the code has survived through the centuries, providing many modern-day scholars with useful information about Babylonian society and how it was structured. Today, the Code of Hammurabi can be seen at the Louvre Museum in Paris.

In ancient Greece, one of the most celebrated early libraries belonged to Aristotle, the famous philosopher who taught Alexander the Great, and was likely housed at his philosophy school, where it could be used by all the students. We know that this library must have been vast because people were writing even long after Aristotle's death of its scope and importance. One writer said that Aristotle "was the first to have put together a collection of books and to have taught the kings of Egypt how to arrange a library." Clearly, Aristotle had developed some kind of system for organizing his many papyrus scrolls (which, unlike our books today, had no spines for displaying titles or author names). His system would have ensured that he and his students were always able to find the scrolls they wanted.

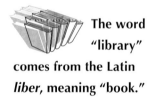 The word "library" comes from the Latin *liber*, meaning "book."

China had libraries as early as 550 B.C., but many early
Chinese writings were reportedly destroyed during the reign of
China's self-appointed first emperor, Shi Huangdi, in the 200s
B.C. In what may be more fiction than fact, it is said that Shi
Huangdi – who's also remembered for beginning construction
on the Great Wall – burned every piece of history, philosophy,
and literature that existed before he came to power. His aim
essentially was to erase the past and write a new history that
would begin in the first year of his reign. Even if the story is
an exaggeration, it seems likely that Shi Huangdi realized,
as so many others would as well, that to hold on to his power,

The Dead Sea Scrolls

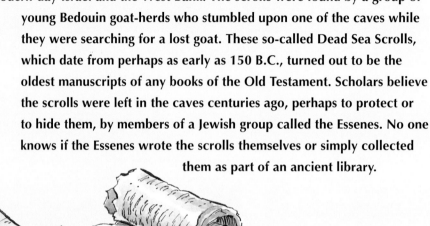

In the middle of the last century, several hundred leather scrolls were discovered in caves alongside the Dead Sea, in modern-day Israel and the West Bank. The scrolls were found by a group of young Bedouin goat-herds who stumbled upon one of the caves while they were searching for a lost goat. These so-called Dead Sea Scrolls, which date from perhaps as early as 150 B.C., turned out to be the oldest manuscripts of any books of the Old Testament. Scholars believe the scrolls were left in the caves centuries ago, perhaps to protect or to hide them, by members of a Jewish group called the Essenes. No one knows if the Essenes wrote the scrolls themselves or simply collected them as part of an ancient library.

he would have to control the literature and intellectual resources of his people.

In Rome, most early libraries were private collections, like Aristotle's. Writers and philosophers and other intellectuals often had large holdings – in fact, a private library was a kind of status symbol – and they would give access to their collections to their friends and colleagues. Most of what we know about these libraries, however, is based only on writings from the time and other second-hand reports. The libraries of ancient Rome, like those in Greece and Egypt, disappeared in the wars and natural disasters that also destroyed so much more of the ancient world.

One library that did survive belonged to a Roman nobleman called Lucius Calpurnius Piso, the father-in-law of Julius Caesar. Piso lived in Herculaneum, a town that, long after his death, was wiped out by the eruption of the volcano Vesuvius, in 79 A.D. Buried under as much as a hundred feet (30 meters)

of volcanic mud and lava that eventually hardened into rock, Piso's villa, including its library, was protected from the ravages of time and nature. In the mid-1700s, the villa was rediscovered. Maneuvering through hand-carved tunnels in long, narrow boats that resembled Venetian gondolas, excavation crews rescued the library from its rocky grave. Along with countless tools, statues, and paintings, the workers found well-preserved wooden shelves and bookcases stacked with about eighteen hundred charred but salvageable papyrus rolls. Today many of these rolls – some little more than lumps of charcoal – can be viewed in Italy's National Archaeological Museum in Naples. Researchers are now trying to decipher the most badly burned using digital imaging technology.

The ABCs of the Alphabet

The history of libraries is closely related to the history of the written word. For thousands of years, people have been recording their ideas and stories of the world around them through a variety of writing systems on a number of different writing materials.

The earliest forms of writing were simple pictures of people, animals, and everyday objects, called pictograms. Around 3000 B.C., the Egyptians developed a more sophisticated writing system known as hieroglyphics. Hieroglyphics were symbols that represented whole words and sounds. Other ancient people, like the Maya of Central America, had similar methods of recording information. As cultures became more dependent upon written records, however, the need for something simpler became obvious, and eventually people began to develop writing systems that allowed whole languages to be put down in just twenty to thirty abstract symbols. The set of characters we write with today, called the Roman alphabet, can be traced to letter shapes first used more than four thousand years ago.

Piso's library would also have been private, for his own use and the enjoyment of his friends. But his son-in-law soon had a different idea. Shortly before his murder in 44 B.C., Julius Caesar announced his plan to build two huge libraries – one for Greek books and one for Latin – and open them to the public. His death halted the plan only temporarily, and by 39 B.C. Rome's first public library had opened its doors.

This library, like all the public ones that followed it, would have focused more on literary works than, for example, legal or medical texts. Reading was something the average Roman did as a hobby – a way to relax and pass the time. In fact, many of Rome's subsequent public libraries were set up in the city's popular bathhouses, which were really almost like modern-day community centers. In addition to their libraries and reading rooms, the bathhouses offered exercise and games rooms, walking paths, and rooms for lectures or small concerts – anything to help overstressed Romans unwind at the end of a long and trying day.

The idea of giving ordinary Romans access to a library was completely new in Caesar's time and shows something of the value placed on the pursuit of knowledge in the ancient world.

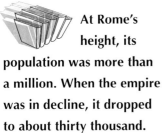 **At Rome's height, its population was more than a million. When the empire was in decline, it dropped to about thirty thousand.**

Unfortunately, the Roman Empire began to decline in the 200s A.D., and by 476 one of the greatest empires the world has ever seen had collapsed. There followed a period in European history when civilization in general faded and much of the knowledge that had come out of ancient societies like Greece and Rome was lost. Fewer people could read and write, learning was no longer valued, and libraries, like so many other cultural institutions, began to disappear. These were the Dark Ages.

CHAPTER TWO

The Darkest Days

When Muslim soldiers conquered Egypt in 642 A.D., many Alexandrians were worried about the fate of their city. The Arabs, they feared, would never appreciate Alexandria's beauty, its impressive architecture, and its rich culture. They were pleasantly surprised, then, when they discovered that these men were not the barbarians they had expected. In fact, one Alexandrian was so encouraged by the new Muslim governor's interest in music and poetry that he dared to ask him what would happen to the thousands of papyrus scrolls held in the Serapeum, the city's second great library. He didn't get the answer he was hoping for, however. "If what is written in [the scrolls] agrees with the Book of God," he was told, "they are not required; if it disagrees, they are not desired. Destroy them therefore." And with that, the scrolls were carried off to be used as fuel in Alexandria's thousands of public bathhouses. There were so many scrolls to burn that they reportedly kept the furnaces going day and night for six solid months.

Most historians now think this tale is untrue, but even if those scrolls were never really turned into fuel, the Serapeum, like its great sister library, was certainly destroyed at some point in time. And it was only one of hundreds, if not thousands,

Alexandria's Fiery End

No one knows for sure what happened to the Library of Alexandria. For centuries, though, most people believed that it was burned to the ground when Julius Caesar set fire to the Egyptian fleet in Alexandria's harbor in 48 B.C. The story was that Caesar torched the ships to prevent his enemies from capturing the great city by sea. But things apparently did not go quite as planned. The wind carried the flames off the ships' masts and onto the buildings along Alexandria's shore, setting the great library and its thousands of fragile papyrus scrolls alight. In what must have seemed like an instant, the Library of Alexandria was gone.

Today, most historians discount this story. They think the library's decline was much slower and less dramatic. It's now widely assumed that a combination of fires, invasions, and simple wear and tear brought about Alexandria's tragic end.

that suffered that fate during the Dark Ages. All over western Europe, libraries were being destroyed or dismantled. One writer sadly observed that "the libraries are closing forever, like tombs."

How did things get to this state? Well, when the Roman Empire began to fall apart, it had neither the money to support its libraries nor the citizens to make use of them. Some libraries were demolished by invading armies, but others simply collapsed from neglect. At the same time, a powerful new religion, Christianity, was on the rise. Church leaders had little interest in preserving the pagan (pre-Christian) literature of ancient Greece and Rome, so they made no effort to save the libraries from ruin. Instead, they began opening libraries of their own, in the churches and monasteries that were just then beginning to emerge all over Europe.

To build the collections of these monastic libraries, the monks who lived there would spend their days laboriously copying out manuscripts by hand. In this way, they safeguarded books in a time when learning and culture were little appreciated. Almost without exception, they were duplicating the Bible and other religious works, but some monasteries did also make copies of writings from ancient Greece and Rome, preserving those works for future generations of readers.

The oldest known copy of the Bible was found in a monastery on the Sinai Peninsula. Dating from the early 300s A.D., this manuscript is now in the collection of the British Library.

The monks' copies were extremely valuable. Not only were they decorated with elaborate, hand-painted designs in bright colors and real gold leaf – which is how these so-called illuminated manuscripts got their name – but each one took hundreds and hundreds of hours to produce. Even the materials they were made from were expensive. It could take dozens of animal hides to prepare the parchment for just one title.

And yet, the care that went into physically creating the illuminated manuscripts did not always also go into copying them. The scribes – from boredom, laziness, or just a lack of knowledge – were sometimes a little on the sloppy side, and their manuscripts were often full of errors. One writer lamented, "Who will discover a cure for the ignorance and vile sloth of these copyists, who spoil everything and turn it to nonsense?"

Perhaps the monks could be forgiven for being a bit careless, however, for working in the scriptorium (writing room) was no easy assignment. The scribes labored away, often for six

Life in the Scriptorium

Most monasteries throughout Europe and in parts of Africa and Asia had scriptoriums. Like the monasteries themselves, the scriptoriums were mostly self-sufficient. Calves and sheep from the monastery grounds provided the skin to make parchment and the leather for book covers, while geese supplied the feathers for quills. The monks even made their own inks.

Within the scriptorium itself, the monks were given different jobs to suit their abilities. Those who simply wrote up the day-to-day business of the monastery, like letters and account books, were called *librarii*. The monks who actually copied the manuscripts were *antiquarii*, while the *illuminators* were the ones who painted all those magnificent, brightly colored designs and illustrations.

or seven hours a day, in rooms that were cold, damp, and dim
(there was a fear that too much light could harm the valuable
manuscripts they were working on). "Those who do not know
how to write do not think it is labor," one monk observed.
"It is true that only three fingers write, but the whole body
toils." While they worked, the scribes were expected to stay
completely silent. When they needed something, they had to
communicate with signs and hand gestures. A monk who wanted
a new manuscript to copy, for example, would pretend to turn
the pages of an imaginary book, while one who needed a pagan
work would scratch himself like a dog.

Each scriptorium produced books mostly for its monastery's
own library. If multiple copies of the same manuscript were
needed, one monk would sometimes read the text aloud to
several others so they could all duplicate it at the same time. A
monastery would also occasionally borrow books from another
scriptorium to copy and add to its own collection, in what was
like an early version of an inter-library loan. Sometimes monks

 **To safeguard
works that
had been forbidden by
the church, librarians of
the Middle Ages sometimes
scratched out or covered
up the names of the authors
and pretended the books
had been written by
someone else.**

Decoding the Codex

It is generally believed that medieval Christian scribes developed the codex, the earliest form of something that we would recognize to this day as a book. To make a codex, a scribe would cut a piece of parchment into sheets, sew the sheets together along one side, and bind them between two scraps of wood. A codex was both more durable and more practical than a scroll. The wooden "covers" protected the parchment from wear, and both sides of the sheets could be filled with writing. Finding specific passages was also less complicated in a codex; a reader could flip back and forth between numbered pages with ease, instead of rolling and unrolling a scroll in a frustrating hunt for the reference he wanted. Today, we "scroll" for references on computer screens, in a digital-age version of those ancient manuscripts. But unlike those ancient readers, modern-day users of online information have the ability to do a keyword search – a simple feature that makes finding references so much easier than in days gone by.

were sent great distances to acquire titles for their monasteries. Abbots from the north of England, for example, routinely traveled as far as Rome in search of books.

Eventually, most monks learned to write in a variety of scripts. They would choose special scripts for each text, just as today's book designers choose from among thousands of different typefaces. The monks also made their manuscripts easier to read and understand by introducing lowercase letters and spaces to show where each word stopped and started. They even began to use some basic punctuation, like the semicolon and a version of the period. Before this, no punctuation existed and most works were written entirely in capital letters.

The collections these monasteries put together helped preserve many important works through what was a dark and dreadful time in western Europe. In the rest of the world, however, culture continued to flourish. While western Europe was growing more primitive, the Byzantine Empire, the Arab world, and China were all producing great art, magnificent buildings, and important works of literature.

Everything Old Is New Again

Many manuscripts from classical antiquity were destroyed or lay unused and hidden from view in monastery and cathedral libraries throughout the Middle Ages. Most would have been lost forever had it not been for the efforts of a famous fourteenth-century Italian poet called Petrarch (whom we'll meet again in the next chapter). When he rediscovered the works of some notable Greek and Roman writers, Petrarch saw that they would still appeal to people of his own time. Inspired, he traveled to monasteries in France, Germany, Italy, and Spain to find and rescue other classical manuscripts that had long been forgotten. Many scholars insist that it is only because of Petrarch that today we can read the writings of Cicero, an important Roman orator (public speaker), and Livy, a great ancient historian, among many others.

In the Islamic world, in particular, there was a deep love of books and indeed learning in general, which is why so many scholars doubt the story that opened this chapter. Muhammad, the founder of Islam, encouraged all his followers to study and even copy out the Quran, the Islamic holy book, as a way of committing it to memory. As a result, Muslims were much more likely than Christians to be able to read and write. They also had an appreciation for the book as a work of art. Baghdad, the center of the Muslim world, was home to numerous calligraphers and illustrators, and these men produced books rivaled in beauty only by the illuminated manuscripts made by the monks in the west.

Although Muhammad pressed his followers to learn to read and write, he himself could not.

At their wealthiest and most powerful, the Muslims had an empire that stretched from Spain all the way to the borders of China. Everywhere they introduced Islam, they also established libraries. At Cordoba, in southern Spain, there was one that reportedly held about half a million volumes. When the library moved to a new building, it apparently took six months just to transport all the books. In Cairo, another large Islamic library had more than two thousand illuminated copies of the Quran.

But the greatest of all Islamic libraries was Baghdad's Bayt al-Hikmah, or House of Wisdom. Founded in about 830 A.D., the House of Wisdom was a center for research and a school for

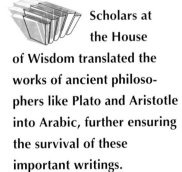 **Scholars at the House of Wisdom translated the works of ancient philosophers like Plato and Aristotle into Arabic, further ensuring the survival of these important writings.**

translation. It was known throughout the world, and probably attracted students from Islamic territories as far away as Europe and Africa. Many scholars actually lived within the library, and they were often given free food and supplies, like paper and ink, as well as access to as many books as they wanted.

The House of Wisdom had a vast collection of religious writings – books about the Quran and about Islam in general – but it also contained important works of mathematics, history, medicine, and philosophy. The chief ruler of Baghdad, called the caliph, paid the salaries of hundreds of employees – librarians to conserve and organize the House of Wisdom's collection; scholars to translate newly acquired works from languages like Greek and Latin into Arabic; calligraphers to make copies of

Byzantine Beginnings

In 395 A.D., in its dying days, the Roman Empire split into two parts – the East Roman Empire, which was ruled from Constantinople, and the West Roman Empire, which remained centered in Rome. The western half was overrun by Germanic invaders in the 400s and finally collapsed in 476. But the eastern half, also called the Byzantine Empire, survived and thrived, preserving much of the art and literature of Greece and Rome, along with many of the political and legal traditions of those ancient societies. In this way, the Byzantine Empire became a bridge between the old, pagan world and the modern, Christian one.

manuscripts and bookbinders to bind them. The caliph also employed agents to roam the world looking for books to purchase. Because he so valued the written word, he paid generously for these volumes, and that sparked a thriving book trade. By the late 800s, Baghdad alone had at least a hundred booksellers.

The other great imperial power of the time was the East Roman Empire, also called the Byzantine Empire. Its capital city, Constantinople (now Istanbul, Turkey), was, like Baghdad, a great cultural center. The Justinian Code, a collection of laws and legal principles, was produced there in the 500s. The code explained and interpreted almost a thousand years of Roman laws, illustrating them with case studies. It became the foundation for the law codes of many countries and is widely considered one of the greatest of all Roman contributions to Western civilization.

The Birth of the Bookmobile?

Libraries were not always stored in buildings. One tenth-century Persian official was so attached to his personal book collection that he took it with him everywhere he went. Grand Vizier Abdul Kassem Ismael used more than five hundred camels to carry the hundred thousand books he owned, in effect creating the first mobile library in history. It is even said that he trained his camel caravan to walk in order so that all his books could be accessed alphabetically!

Constantinople was also home to Hagia Sophia, a magnificent domed cathedral that still attracts tourists to the city, and to three significant libraries, including the Imperial Library.

Founded in the early fourth century by Constantine the Great, Rome's first Christian emperor, the Imperial Library survived for more than a thousand years, until the capture of Constantinople by Turkish soldiers in 1453. But the success of the library rose and fell with the fortunes of its empire, which was, at various points in its history, besieged by Germans, Slavs,

The Crusades

The Crusades were a series of Christian military expeditions between 1096 and 1270 A.D. Thousands volunteered to take part – from priests and kings to peasants and children. The Crusaders were determined to recapture the Holy Land (a region in what is now Israel that is sacred to Christians) from the hands of the Muslims. They also wanted to expand the power and influence of the Christian church.

There were eight Crusades in total, but most were largely unsuccessful. The Crusaders failed to permanently retake control of the Holy Land, and infighting between Christians from western Europe and those from the Byzantine Empire stirred bad feelings and hostility between the two groups. The Crusades did lead to more contact between the West and the East, however, increasing trade and commerce and enriching European life in countless ways.

Persians, Muslims, and Serbs. The end for both the library and the empire almost came in the 1200s, when Christian knights and noblemen from western Europe reached Constantinople as part of the Fourth Crusade. The city was overrun, and most of the books of the Imperial Library were either destroyed or sold off to Italian merchants who recognized their value.

When the Turks finally conquered Byzantium once and for all in 1453, the empire was so weakened that its demise was almost a non-event. The Turks resumed the Crusaders' practice of selling off books from the few remaining Byzantine libraries, and it's said that the trade in Greek manuscripts thrived for the next hundred years. Most of the great Muslim libraries had also been wiped out by that time, falling victim to fires, floods, and rivalries between different Islamic sects. But the worst damage came when the vast and brutal armies of Asia's Mongol Empire swept through in the 1200s. When they reached Baghdad in 1258, the Mongols reportedly destroyed all of its libraries in less than a week. So many books were tossed into the waters

of the Tigris River that they supposedly formed a bridge that reached from one bank to the other.

Yet despite all the destruction and ruin, the increased contact between East and West – particularly through the two centuries of the Crusades – had some benefits. During their time in the territories of the Byzantine Empire and in the Holy Land, Crusaders were exposed to writings and ideas that had been lost to western Europe. The trade in books, seen first in Baghdad and later throughout Byzantium, also brought many valuable manuscripts back to the West. In fact, it's said that of all the Greek texts known today, 75 percent come from Byzantine copies, not from their Greek originals. For Europeans, the flow of manuscripts and ideas between cultures opened a long-forgotten door to the classical world. While the decline of the Byzantine Empire marked the sad end of a once great civilization, it was also the beginning of one of the finest periods of cultural advancement the world has ever seen. It's a period we call the Renaissance.

CHAPTER THREE

A Golden Age

In the mid-1400s, a German goldsmith living in the town of Mainz came up with a brilliant idea. He realized that he could take tools and technologies that were already being used by winemakers, painters, and even his fellow goldsmiths and turn them into something new that the world desperately needed. To bring his idea to life, he began to teach himself all he could about the presses that winemakers used to crush grapes and the black inks that artists in Belgium were making for their canvases. Then he combined that information with everything he already knew about the goldsmith's punch, a tool for making signature marks on jewelry and other goldwork. The machine that emerged from all those bits and pieces was the printing press, and the man who created it was Johannes Gutenberg.

Gutenberg is often called the inventor of printing, but that honor actually belongs to the Chinese. Centuries before Gutenberg came along, they were carving whole pages of text and images into wood blocks, covering the blocks with ink, and pressing them onto paper to make copies. But because there was so little information passing between China and the rest of the world at that time, people outside the country didn't know that printing and other technologies existed there.

How Gutenberg's Printing Press Worked

Gutenberg took all the letters of the alphabet and cast them in metal to make movable type. These letters could be put together in combinations to form words, in words to form lines, and in lines to form whole pages of type. Once a complete page had been assembled, the type-setter would lock the lines together to create a solid unit called a form. He'd then take the form over to the printing press, ink it, slip a sheet of paper into a paper holder, and fold the holder over top of the form. Next, he'd slide the form under a heavy wooden block called a platen. Using a lever to turn a giant wooden screw, the typesetter would lower the platen onto the form, pressing the paper against the type and transferring the ink, and therefore the words in the form, to the sheet. If he wanted to make another copy, he'd simply raise the platen, pull out the form, replace the printed sheet with a blank one, and repeat the process. Gutenberg's press, which was both faster and more accurate than copying by hand, could print about three hundred pages a day.

paper holder

platen

form

inking ball

lever

On top of that, the Chinese printing system was far from perfect. The wood blocks were not very durable and couldn't be printed from once they began to wear down. And because each block was an entire page of manuscript, it could only be used to make copies of that one unique page. Each new page required a whole new block of its own.

The key to making printing more practical lay in something Gutenberg *did* invent. He cast each individual letter of the alphabet in metal, creating something called movable type. These letters could be put together to make a page of text, then taken apart and used again to make a totally different page. They lasted longer than words carved in wood and could be used in endless combinations.

 It would have taken Gutenberg at least two years to produce the three hundred copies he made of his famous Bible, the first book to come off his printing press. More than five hundred years later, about forty of those copies still exist.

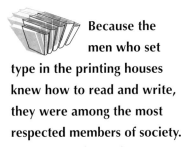 **Because the men who set type in the printing houses knew how to read and write, they were among the most respected members of society.**

Many people feel that movable type was the most important invention in the history of Western civilization. It certainly had a tremendous impact on the countries and citizens of Europe. Before the 1400s, few Europeans could read or write. Most information was passed by word of mouth, so it was unreliable and took a long time to circulate. Even people who could read had trouble getting accurate information. Hand-copied books were often filled with errors, as we saw in the previous chapter. And because they took a long, long time to produce, they were rare and too expensive for most ordinary people to afford.

Printing from movable type changed all that. It came at a time when more people were learning to read and the demand for books was exploding. Europe was transforming itself into a more open, democratic society, a place where knowledge was no longer restricted to the top citizens. Thanks to Gutenberg and men like him, anyone who could read – no matter his

Borrowers Beware

Early Renaissance librarians had to protect the books in their care from decay, fire, and vandalism, as well as theft. The incentive for keeping the collection safe was great – some librarians were made personally responsible for books that were defaced or went missing. The job description for one obligated him to "preserve the books from damp and vermin, as well as from the hands of trifling, ignorant, dirty, and tasteless persons."

To safeguard their book collections – and perhaps also their jobs – many librarians established strong rules to try to keep readers in line. In cathedral libraries, notices warned that anyone who stole or even damaged a book could face excommunication (expulsion from the church). One particularly fierce sign even promised that any library user who attempted to "carry away one of these books by theft, by fraud, or in any other manner" would have his name "struck from the book of the living"!

background or his position in life – suddenly had access to more information than ever before. This meant that new discoveries and ideas could spread more easily, and that people could form their own opinions and begin to think for themselves.

The impact of movable type on libraries was just as profound. In the early years of the Renaissance, before Gutenberg's press gained wide acceptance, most book collections were still to be found in Catholic monasteries or cathedrals. These libraries were not much like the ones we visit today. They were stocked mostly with religious texts and were for the use of theology students and the monks whose hard work in the scriptoriums helped fill the shelves. Each one of their hand-copied books represented years of work and was almost irreplaceable, so the collections were extremely valuable. To guard against theft, librarians used long chains to fasten their books to rods that ran along the front of the shelves. Readers could lift the books down to a desktop but could move no farther away than the chain allowed. Library users were also sometimes required to hand over volumes of their own as a kind of collateral. (They would get these back when they had returned the

The Protestant Reformation

On Halloween Day, 1517, a German monk named Martin Luther went to his local church and nailed to its door a paper called the Ninety-five Theses. This was an attack on corruption within the Roman Catholic Church, and in particular on the sale of indulgences, which were slips of paper that church-goers could buy to excuse themselves from their sins.

When Luther refused to give in to pressure from Catholic leaders and take back what he had written, he was expelled from the church. But many people shared his point of view, and soon he had a great number of followers and was leading a movement known as Protestantism. The Protestant Reformation caused a permanent split between Catholics and Protestants, but it also led to many improvements within the Roman Catholic Church. Perhaps most important of all, it helped transform Europe into a more tolerant, literate, open society.

library's books undamaged.) Occasionally, they were made to swear an oath before they were allowed access to books in the collection.

With the sudden availability of printed books, however, and the rise of a religious and cultural movement known as the Protestant Reformation, libraries began to change drastically. Protestants in northern and central Europe started to dismantle many cathedral and monastery libraries and distribute their books among the universities that had been established in most major cities at the start of the Renaissance. Protestants had a great belief in education, and they thought of universities as training grounds not just for clergymen, like the Catholic monasteries had been, but for doctors and lawyers and public servants. They wanted their libraries to be more accessible, to be open to readers from all walks of life. As affordable, easy-to-replace printed books gradually took the spot of hand-written manuscripts on the shelves, that began to become possible.

What Was Humanism?

Renaissance humanism began in fourteenth-century Italy and grew out of a revival of interest in Greek and Latin classical literature. Humanists believed that the writers of ancient Rome and Greece could teach them all they needed to know about leading a moral, virtuous, and human-focused life.

The humanist program of study centered around subjects like poetry, history, philosophy, and grammar. As the movement took hold, wealthy families began to hire humanist tutors to instruct their children in these areas. With the arrival of Gutenberg's press and the growing spread of printed materials, humanist values broke through class barriers and began to trickle down to the less well-to-do. Those values – a belief in the importance of the individual, and in the principles of democracy and reason – helped erode the authority of the church and set the stage for the Enlightenment.

Even the type of books the libraries were stocking was changing. With all the new titles it was producing, the printing press had helped spark a renewed interest in history, poetry, and the literature of the classical world, and this interest eventually grew into a cultural movement called humanism. The Italian poet Petrarch was one of the first important humanist leaders, and as we saw in the previous chapter, he made it his mission to rescue texts from the often neglected and sometimes squalid monastery libraries of Europe – and inspired others to do the same. Soon humanists were traveling far and wide to find and recover the most accurate versions of classical manuscripts. These they turned over to printers so they could make copies that were free of errors.

Finding those accurate versions in the days of hand-copying was sometimes quite a challenge, however. Petrarch once suggested that ancient writers who returned to life in his time would not have been able to recognize their own works, because the copies were so filled with mistakes. "There is no check upon these copyists, selected without examination or test of their capacity," he complained. Other humanists were appalled by the way the manuscripts they unearthed had been treated in the monasteries. One claimed he heard the books

One Italian nobleman had five men whose only job was to read aloud to him during meals.

calling, "Do not allow me through neglect to be entirely destroyed here; save me from these chains!" Most viewed the monasteries as prisons and the books as captive inmates. They bought, borrowed, and sometimes stole titles in their quest to liberate them.

Not all of these newly "liberated" manuscripts found their way into the hands of printers or the collections of universities, however. The Renaissance was also a golden age for private libraries. Just as they were in Julius Caesar's day, libraries once again became status symbols, and many prosperous, powerful people began to amass large book collections. Cosimo de' Medici, a wealthy banker who ruled Florence, Italy, in the early 1400s, had one of the most famous private libraries, a collection that he hoped might one day rival the legendary Library of Alexandria. Over time, his collection became so vast that he was able to create a second library and open it to artists and scholars. This was, in fact, the first library for public use built since Roman times, and Cosimo added others as his collection continued to grow.

The librarian who oversaw Cosimo's collection, Tommaso Parentucelli, was a highly religious man who was chosen to lead the Roman Catholic Church in 1447. As Pope Nicholas V, he invited Catholic pilgrims to come to Rome and give money to the church. He then used those vast sums to pay agents to travel Europe in search of manuscripts. He even bought books from the Imperial Library in Constantinople when that city fell in 1453.

Although the printing press was invented around the time of Nicholas V's reign, it didn't come into wider general use until the 1500s. Fifteenth-century book lovers like Pope Nicholas and Cosimo de' Medici still expanded their collections just as those medieval monks had done centuries earlier: they borrowed volumes from others and had them copied by hand. Nicholas V kept scribes on his staff to duplicate manuscripts that were loaned to him, and he even brought scholars from Constantinople to translate Greek works into Latin. Those books became the core of the Vatican Library, which is to this day one of the great libraries of the Western world.

After the death of Nicholas V in 1455, the Vatican Library continued to grow, though sometimes by less honorable means. In 1508, Pope Leo X sent one monastery a much less valuable printed version of a book in exchange for a handwritten manuscript the monks had apparently not intended the pope to keep. "We have sent a copy of the revised and printed book in a beautiful binding, that [the monks] may place it in their library as a substitute for the one taken from it," he wrote to the abbot. Then he boldly added, "[We hope] that they may understand that the [theft] has done them far more good than harm."

Pope Leo's letter tells us that hand-copied books were still held in higher esteem than printed books. But soon the printing press was producing volumes that were more affordable and more accurate than hand-copied manuscripts could ever be. Books that once took years of laborious effort to duplicate were being issued in the hundreds. The flood of printed matter had begun, and more and more libraries started to spring up to accommodate all that new material. Soon, libraries were being

Librarians of the 1600s were expected to remain single. Marriage was considered too much of a distraction to leave them time to perform their duties.

Oxford's First Library

Duke Humphrey, the youngest brother of King Henry V, gave Oxford University a great collection of his manuscripts in 1411, and the university built a library to house them. Before Humphrey made his donation, Oxford owned very few books, and most of those it did own were kept away from students and faculty in locked chests. Humphrey's gift helped establish the university as an important center of learning.

Unfortunately, Oxford had no funds to maintain the library after the duke's death. Books were vandalized, and some were sold to bookbinders for the value of their parchment. When Protestantism swept through England, things only got worse. According to one unconfirmed account, all of Duke Humphrey's remaining books but one were tossed into a bonfire in the university's main courtyard as part of an effort to rid Oxford of all traces of Roman Catholicism. The duke himself fared far worse. Arrested on suspicion of plotting against his nephew, King Henry VI, he died in prison in 1447.

The Bodleian's spectacular architecture has made it a favorite with filmmakers. It has even doubled as the Hogwarts Library in the Harry Potter films.

housed in their own separate buildings, instead of just in rooms or wings of larger facilities. When new colleges and universities were founded, which was happening at an extraordinary rate, library buildings were included in the original plans.

Many of the greatest libraries of Europe were born at this time, including the Bodleian Library of England's Oxford University. Founded in 1602, the Bodleian was named for Sir Thomas Bodley, a former Oxford student who made it his

Deposit Libraries and the National Memory

In 1610, Thomas Bodley approached the Stationers' Company, a guild to which all printers belonged, and negotiated an agreement that entitled the Bodleian to one free copy of every book printed in England. This arrangement was really a forerunner of legal deposit, a modern law that requires publishers to place free copies of their books in their national libraries. Through legal deposit, a national library is able to create as full a record as possible of a country's literary life – its history, its technical and scientific achievements, its poetry and fiction – thereby preserving the collective memory of all its citizens.

mission to resurrect the university's original library. As a scholar and later a diplomat in the service of Queen Elizabeth I, Bodley traveled all over Europe. On his journeys, he came in contact with many rich, powerful, and well-educated people, and he used his diplomatic skills to persuade them to donate books to the university. By the time of his death in 1613, his library housed six thousand books and manuscripts. The majority of those were in Latin, the language of scholars, but Bodley also acquired titles in Greek, Hebrew, Arabic, Turkish, and Persian. He even added books and manuscripts in Chinese, despite the fact that no one at Oxford could read them!

His passion for acquiring manuscripts in various ancient and sacred languages made the Bodleian the first internationally significant library in England. Today, it is still considered by many to be the greatest university library in the world. The contemporary Bodleian now contains nine million items on 109 miles (176 kilometers) of shelving.

Just thirty-six years after Bodley opened his library, in 1638, Rev. John Harvard of Cambridge, Massachusetts, gave his collection of four hundred books – a substantial private library for the New World at that time – to a fledgling local university. The administrators were so grateful for the gift that they named the school Harvard College in his honor. Several decades later, ten Connecticut church leaders donated books from their own collections to start a school that eventually became Yale

Thomas Bodley refused to include any of William Shakespeare's plays in his library's collection because he thought they were frivolous. The Bodleian began to acquire Shakespeare's work in 1635, after Bodley's death, and it now boasts one of the most valuable Shakespearean collections in the world.

 The Harvard
University
library is the world's largest
scholarly library. It now has
more than twelve million
volumes in its collection.

University. As each man laid his gift on the table, he reportedly said, "I give these books for the founding of a College in this Colony."

A few dozen – or even a few hundred – books may not seem like much to us today, but those gifts were essential to getting these schools off the ground. One early president of Princeton University called books "the most ornamental and useful furniture of a College, and the most proper and valuable fund with which it can be endowed." In a struggling new nation, where the opportunities for apprenticeships (on-the-job training) were not as plentiful as they were in Europe, universities quickly assumed a central role. Their libraries were where most of America's first doctors, lawyers, and businessmen learned their craft. Soon, however, there would emerge the idea that books should not be reserved for a privileged few.

CHAPTER FOUR

Into the New World

Benjamin Franklin, the great American statesman, inventor, and signer of the Declaration of Independence, knew how important it was to have access to good books. He thought of reading as a door to wisdom that was never shut, and he once said that libraries would make "the common tradesmen and farmers [in the Thirteen Colonies] as intelligent as most gentlemen from other countries."

But in the 1700s, when Franklin lived, books were hard to come by in America. Very few printers had set up shop, so books were rare and expensive, and no public lending libraries had yet been established. Unless they had the money to have volumes sent over from England, colonists had to make do with whatever books they'd brought with them when they first came to the New World.

To give himself and others access to more reading material, Franklin came up with the idea of combining his own book collection with the collections of others. He approached the members of the Junto, a debating club he'd founded, and suggested they all move their books to a central location, creating a small library that would give each member, he argued, "the advantage of using the books of all the other members, which would be nearly as beneficial as if each owned the whole."

The Junto's library didn't last long – most members found it inconvenient not to have instant, at-home access to their own books – but it did plant in Franklin's mind the idea of pooling individual resources to benefit a larger group of people. Soon, he wrote, "I set on foot my first project of a public nature, that of a subscription library."

In 1731, Franklin and several friends created the Library Company of Philadelphia, the first American subscription library. In a subscription library, people paid membership fees, and those fees were used to buy books, which members could then borrow free of charge. In the case of Franklin's library, fifty initial subscribers paid membership dues of forty shillings apiece and another ten shillings a year in fees after that. (Forty shillings was about two months' pay for a sailor at the time, and the annual fees were more than the weekly wage of an unskilled laborer.) With that money, Franklin was able to order books and magazines from England and add other titles whenever he visited Europe. The books were housed in the Pennsylvania State House (now Independence Hall) and circulated freely among the library's members.

Benjamin Franklin's subscription library eventually formed the basis for Philadelphia's modern public library system.

The Libraries of New Spain

Libraries in Latin America existed long before those in the rest of the New World. Spanish conquerors and missionary priests first brought large book collections to several countries, including Mexico, Guatemala, and Peru, in the 1500s. Reading was so highly valued by the Spanish, in fact, that when a man named Antonio de Mendoza was appointed the first viceroy of Mexico, in 1535, he brought an entire printing press across the ocean from Spain. The following year, that press produced the first book printed in the New World, a Spanish translation of a Latin text. For several decades, before the craft came to the American colonies, Mexico was the only place in the New World where a book could be printed.

Franklin called the Library Company of Philadelphia "the mother of all North American subscription libraries," and not without good reason. His concept was copied all over the Thirteen Colonies, in important colonial cities like Boston and Newport, Rhode Island. By the time the American Revolution began, in 1775, there were dozens of subscription libraries in America, serving everyone from farmers to merchants. Members could borrow novels, biographies, and history books, as well as more practical works on architecture, farming, and the law. Some collections even contained volumes on etiquette and gentlemanly conduct!

Not everyone had access to a subscription library in their own community, of course, or could afford the annual membership dues. To serve those people, many shopkeepers began opening commercial lending libraries in their stores. Retailers like stationers and dry-goods merchants would stock their shelves with books and rent them out to customers for a modest fee, much like modern-day video stores do with movies. It was a clever way for tradespeople to both fill a gap

A Palace for the People

In 1854, the Boston Public Library, the first publicly supported library in a major North American city, opened for business in two rooms on the ground floor of a former schoolhouse. Thanks to many large gifts of both books and money, the library grew quickly, and soon it had the world's largest publicly circulating collection. By the 1880s, the Boston city council had concluded that such an important institution deserved its own grand new building. Designed by the architect Charles McKim, the resulting structure was modeled on an Italian Renaissance palace. Over the front entrance, McKim inscribed the words "Built by the people and dedicated to the advancement of learning."

The new building was full of innovations, including a newspaper room and the first children's department ever set up in a public library. Forward-thinking ideas like these helped cement the Boston Public Library's reputation for pioneering work in the development of library services.

Today, part of the Central Library is still housed in McKim's spectacular building on Boston's famous Copley Square. It's just one part of a large and important library system that serves more than two million patrons a year through twenty-six separate branches.

in the marketplace and encourage more people to come through their shop doors.

Around this time, there began to emerge the idea that libraries had an important role to play in a newly established, democratic society. Supporters believed that libraries would "promote orderly and virtuous habits, diffuse knowledge and the desire for knowledge, [and] improve the scientific skill." They would provide working people like farmers and office clerks – people who often didn't have much opportunity for formal education – with the information they needed to acquire new skills and become better, more prosperous citizens. In the days before television, radio, and the movies, libraries were also viewed as a welcome distraction from less respectable entertainments like gambling and drinking.

The notion that libraries could help a nation's more needy citizens improve and advance themselves led to the establishment of what were called mechanics' institutes. These organizations were designed specifically for working-class citizens, especially factory laborers (known as mechanics), tradesmen, and apprentices. As well as providing members with access to books, the mechanics' institutes often housed small museums, sponsored lectures, and offered skills training. The idea was for laborers from all different trades to come together and learn from one another.

The mechanics' institutes grew out of a British movement to address the educational needs of the working classes. Between the 1820s and the 1860s, hundreds of these institutes were established in England, the United States, and Canada. There were mechanics' institutes in Philadelphia (it still exists today, as the Franklin Institute); Baltimore; St. John's, Newfoundland; and Toronto, among many, many other places. These were still not true public libraries – their collections were not made freely available to everyone in the community – but they were the only place most working-class North Americans could turn to for organized courses and lessons.

Thanks to the mechanics' institutes, many hard-working citizens were able to move up in society. One who certainly

The Fairer Sex

The first woman to work in a North American library was Mrs. A. B. Harnden, who was hired in 1856 for the Boston Athenaeum. This was no small accomplishment: many people felt that libraries often housed "the corrupter portions of the polite literature," and therefore that the presence of women would cause "frequent embarrassment to modest men." But in the 1850s, the world was beginning to change. Women were demanding the right to be educated and the freedom to work at any job for which they were able to qualify. Despite some early opposition, people soon began to view librarianship as an acceptable profession for "respectable" women.

Of course, getting that foot in the door was only half the battle. Women still had to accept much lower salaries than their male colleagues received for the same work. Still, their efforts slowly began to be appreciated – in a way. In 1887, the first president of the American Library Association told a group of English librarians that female employees "soften our atmosphere, they lighten our labour, they are equal to our work, and for the money they cost – they are infinitely better than equivalent salaries will produce in the other sex."

Thank goodness, this attitude has disappeared. Today, men and women work side by side and enjoy equal opportunities.

benefited from them was a young Scottish teenager who'd immigrated to Pittsburgh, Pennsylvania, in 1847. As a clerk and telegraph operator for the Pennsylvania Railroad, Andrew Carnegie made frequent use of the local Mechanics' and Apprentices' Library, gathering there with his friends to read through the small collection and discuss the books. Carnegie – who went on to make millions in the steel industry and was at one time the world's richest man – never forgot how that modest library had enriched his life. It had, he later said, "opened to me the intellectual wealth of the world."

Because he'd started working at age twelve, Carnegie had very little formal schooling, and the mechanics' institute he used represented a rare opportunity for self-improvement at no charge. He objected strongly, therefore, when the administrators of the library decided to ask patrons to pay an annual membership fee. He battled the librarians both privately and in the local newspaper, until eventually the fee was waived.

This minor skirmish taught Carnegie a lesson he never for-

Every Carnegie library was originally designed with a prominent lamppost out front, a symbol of enlightenment. Over the doors of many branches were carved the words "Let there be light."

got about the importance of publicly supported institutions like libraries, museums, and art galleries. "The best means of benefiting a community," he asserted, "is to place within its reach the ladders upon which the aspiring can rise." When he sold off his steel company and retired, in 1901, he began to devote himself to doing exactly that, giving away millions of dollars to establish free public libraries throughout the English-speaking world. "I choose free libraries as the best agencies for improving the masses of the people," he later explained, "because they . . . only help those who help themselves." He added, "They reach the aspiring, and open to these the chief treasures of the world – those stored up in books." In the end, he gave away the equivalent of $3 billion – about 80 percent of his wealth – to build more than two thousand public libraries.

Where to Look

Over the centuries, librarians have struggled with the problem of how best to organize their collections to make the books easy to retrieve. In the great Islamic libraries, including the House of Wisdom, the system was simple: the book with the "noblest" subject matter came first and all others followed behind. Books on religion, of course, were considered the noblest of all; they were followed by literature and history, while subjects like medicine and mathematics were a distant third. Within these categories, the book that contained the most references to the Quran came first. A similar system was used in Catholic monastery libraries, where the Bible was the most important work. Writings by early church leaders, studies of the Bible, stories of saints' lives, and secular (non-Christian) literature followed, in that order.

Today, many libraries use the Dewey Decimal System to organize their book collections. That's certainly not the only method that exists, however. Some very large libraries, like university and scholarly libraries, use the more detailed Library of Congress Classification, while scientific and technical libraries tend to prefer something called the Universal Decimal System. Other nations sometimes have their own unique systems. In China, there's even a method for organizing books according to the principles of Marxist philosophy!

Andrew Carnegie ushered in a second golden age in library history, and libraries have been prospering ever since. Over time, different types have emerged to meet different needs. Along with public libraries, there are academic and school libraries, special libraries, and national libraries. Special libraries house specific material that wouldn't normally be found in more general libraries, such as medical texts or law books. They are often attached to institutions like hospitals or museums, but many belong to large companies and some are even privately owned. MTV, for example, has a library of millions of songs and music videos. The Hockey Hall of Fame, in Toronto, has a library that includes player files and programs from Stanley Cup games dating back to 1902.

National libraries, as we saw in the previous chapter, exist to collect and preserve a country's literary output. Almost every nation in the world has established a national library. Some of the most comprehensive — like the British Library and France's

Canada's national library, founded in 1953, recently merged with the nation's archives to create Library and Archives Canada. Some items in its collection date back to the early 1500s.

The Dewey Decimal System

As libraries added more and more books to their collections, it became clear that there needed to be a better system of classifying and organizing them. In 1876, a young library assistant named Melvil Dewey came up with the idea of assigning numbers to books to represent different categories of learning. Still used today by most public libraries in North America, this system became known as the Dewey Decimal Classification.

Dewey's organizing system divides books into ten main groups. All books on religion get a number somewhere between 200 and 299, for example, while books of geography and history fall somewhere between 900 and 999. These ten broad general categories are then divided into subcategories. For instance, books on the history of the ancient world are numbered from 930 to 939. As the topics get more specific, Dewey's numbers do as well – the history of ancient Egypt is 932, the history of ancient Greece is 938. When the categories become very specific, a decimal place is added.

What makes the Dewey Decimal System so useful is that it groups together all books on the same subject. That's great for you if you're doing a project on ancient Egypt and are looking for books to use for your research. All you have to do is find the shelves numbered 932 and browse away.

national library, the Bibliothèque nationale de France — have been building their collections for many hundreds of years, so they've been able to create an irreplaceable historical record. Even those that have been around for a much shorter period of time have often been able to put together remarkable collections. For instance, the world's largest national library, the American Library of Congress, got its start in 1800, when Thomas Jefferson sold the six thousand books in his private library to the government for the use of members of Congress. Today, the Library of Congress has about 115 million items in its collection, including books, maps, photographs, films, and sound recordings. Like all national libraries, the Library of Congress is exploring new ways of making its important collection more readily available to people who want to see it.

Around the globe, people have taken the "books for all" philosophy of Andrew Carnegie, Benjamin Franklin, and others like them and given it life in unusual and surprising forms.

In northeastern Kenya, for example, camels lumber across the
desert sands – just as they did in the days of that tenth-century
vizier in Persia – to bring books to rural villages where illiteracy
is a crippling problem. Donkeys make up a mobile library in
the southern African country of Zimbabwe. Equipped with
solar panels and battery packs, the donkeys carry fax, e-mail,
and Internet services to remote communities, connecting
isolated villagers with the outside world.

In Thailand, the navy joined forces with the government's
ministry of education to create a library out of a decommis-
sioned ship. Stocked with more than two thousand books,
video- and audiotapes, and games and toys for children, this
floating library patrols the Chao Phraya River five days a week,
bringing books and information to some of Bangkok's poorest
citizens. A bookboat also sails the Baltic Sea to carry library
services to the inaccessible islands of an archipelago east of

Turning the Pages

Many national libraries are exploring new ways of making their rarest and most valuable books and manuscripts available to all who want to see them. One of the most exciting of these projects is the British Library's Turning the Pages initiative. Using digitization, animation, and touch-screen technologies, this project allows visitors to the library's website to virtually turn the pages of several important works that are ordinarily hidden away under glass.

Simply by logging on (at www.bl.uk/onlinegallery/ttp/ttpbooks.html), you can see such amazing things as a sixteenth-century atlas of Europe, an early and extremely influential book on human anatomy, and a seventh-century copy of the Gospels. You can open up the notebooks of Leonardo da Vinci and look at his actual drawings of mirrors, weights and pulleys, and musical instruments. Or you can read through the entire text of Lewis Carroll's original handwritten manuscript for *Alice's Adventures in Wonderland*.

Stockholm, Sweden. The residents of Sweden's remotest communities flock to the old passenger steamer to enjoy films, lectures, musical performances, and readings by prominent authors who go along for the ride.

People who believe in the power of the written word will do almost anything to connect others with books. Around the world, librarians fight to protect readers' rights and to ensure that Benjamin Franklin's door to wisdom never closes. This commitment to knowledge has inspired many librarians to explore emerging technologies and create learning opportunities for future generations. Computers, the Internet, databases, and other new media are transforming our culture – just as inventions like writing and paper and Gutenberg's printing press once did – and today the world of libraries is changing in ways that once could never have been imagined.

CHAPTER FIVE

Back to the Future

On October 16, 2002, more than a millennium and a half after its famous ancestor disappeared off the face of the earth, a new Alexandria library opened its doors. The eleven-story, state-of-the-art structure, called the Bibliotheca Alexandrina, occupies the same spot where it's believed the great ancient library once stood. But that's where the similarities end.

While the original Library of Alexandria prided itself on having a copy of every document known to exist, the new library is much more modest in scale. In fact, at its opening, it had only two hundred thousand volumes on its shelves – about half the number of documents of the ancient library, and a mere fraction of the twenty million books held by the American Library of Congress, the world's largest library.

Instead of trying to become a new version of what its sister library was in its day, the Bibliotheca Alexandrina has focused on specific areas, like providing services for children and the visually impaired, building special collections on the history of Egypt and the Middle East, and maintaining an archive of every web page on every existing website from 1996 to the present day. With this last initiative, the Bibliotheca Alexandrina hopes to create a universal digital library that can be accessed by any

The exterior walls of the new Alexandria library are etched with letters from most of the world's alphabets, symbolizing the mixing of cultures and ideas that takes place inside.

person anywhere in the world. Currently, this digital collection includes more than ten billion web pages, two thousand hours of television broadcasting, and a thousand archival films.

The Bibliotheca Alexandrina is only one of several new libraries that have been built around the world at the start of the twenty-first century. Cutting-edge institutions have been constructed in many major North American cities – including Seattle, Washington; Salt Lake City, Utah; and Montreal, Quebec – and in other communities across the globe. These new libraries have cast off their slightly dusty reputations and become centers for new media and information technologies. At Salt Lake City's main branch, for example, customers can use the training lab to learn basic software skills, surf the Internet free of charge, search library databases, and create PowerPoint presentations. People can also bring in their own laptops and get online using the library's wireless Internet connection. Singapore, meanwhile, has been experimenting with so-called lifestyle libraries – branches that cater to particular age groups or people with special interests. A library in one of the city's trendiest shopping malls, for example, offers graphic novels and hip music in a café setting. Other small neighborhood branches are specially for children. In Malaysia, the new Kuala Lumpur Public Library, which opened in 2004, features a virtual reality section where patrons can experience aquarium life, explore human anatomy, and learn more about their own city. In another section, portable audio players are provided for readers who want to listen to their favorite music while they read.

Far from being made extinct by the Internet, CDs, and e-books, libraries are adapting to changing conditions and expanding their role, earning new customers in the process. Sometimes this has meant approaching traditional services in untraditional ways. Many libraries now offer drive-thru service, where customers can pick up pre-ordered books, pay overdue fines, and even ask a reference question! And in places like the award-winning Seattle Public Library, it is already possible to use something called radio frequency

In the past ten years, the number of annual visits to Singapore's libraries has more than quadrupled – from 5.7 million to 31 million.

The New Andrew Carnegie

Bill Gates, the co-founder of Microsoft and co-chair of the Bill & Melinda Gates Foundation, has taken over where Andrew Carnegie left off, becoming the most generous private supporter of public libraries. The Gates Foundation has provided millions of dollars to libraries around the world to support initiatives that increase free access to computers and the Internet for residents in low-income and disadvantaged communities. Since its inception, the foundation has awarded grants to programs in Chile, Mexico, Finland, and China, among many other countries. In 2005, the foundation gave its Access to Learning Award to a program in Bangladesh that uses converted boats, solar panels, and mobile phones to bring Internet access to remote villages in the northern part of the country.

In the United States, the Bill & Melinda Gates Foundation has placed thousands of computers in libraries throughout all fifty states, and it has also supported computer-literacy efforts for Native communities in the American southwest. In Canada, the foundation has provided funding in all thirteen provinces and territories, allowing library staff to purchase more computers, set up training labs, and move up to high-speed Internet connections.

Just as our ancestors depended on Carnegie's libraries for the books and newspapers they needed to master new skills in an adopted country, today's digital immigrants need libraries to help them flourish in our information-driven world. The Bill & Melinda Gates Foundation's commitment to providing Internet access, software, digital resources, and learning tools to public libraries is helping to bring people and technology closer together.

identification (RFID) technology to scan your own library card and check out materials by yourself. Soon, you'll even be able to retrieve your pre-ordered books from a slot as easily as you can pull a candy bar from a vending machine. Developments like these will give librarians more time to spend helping patrons and developing new services.

More than 95 percent of public libraries in the United States and Canada offer free Internet access.

These initiatives are paying off in a big way. Between 1990 and 2001, the number of visits made to libraries in the United States more than doubled. Libraries are doing a booming business in Canada as well. In Toronto – the city with the busiest library system in North America – more than 1.5 million registered borrowers checked out close to 30 million items in 2004.

Library use has also exploded in Bogotá, Colombia, where a program called Biblored has been bringing improved services and free Internet access to citizens since 2001. The network's three newly built central libraries and sixteen renovated neighborhood libraries welcome about two hundred thousand users a month. With nothing more than a free library card, patrons can read books, magazines, and newspapers; surf the Internet; or upgrade their skills with computer classes – all in a peaceful, safe environment. In a city with the highest murder rate in the world – where two-thirds of the citizens live below the poverty line – these libraries are like safe ports in a storm. "It was important for the libraries to be a symbol of hope for the city," said Enrique Peñalosa, Bogotá's former mayor. "Every citizen is invited to use them and to be well treated. To feel important just because he or she is a Colombian."

In other parts of the world – especially in countries where there aren't many libraries and opportunities for schooling are limited – people are exploring new ways to use technology

The African Digital Library

The freely available African Digital Library (www.africandl.org.za/) has a collection of about eight thousand electronic books that can be accessed through any Internet-ready computer on the African continent. The ADL has resources in all areas, but its focus is on subjects like economics, technology, and computers. The idea is to provide Africans with the information they need to hone their skills and expand their businesses, thereby creating new opportunities and fighting the poverty that has plagued parts of the continent. It's a way of providing books and information – and learning opportunities – while avoiding the high cost of constructing and maintaining bricks-and-mortar library buildings.

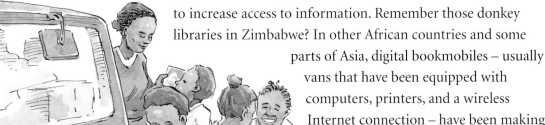

to increase access to information. Remember those donkey libraries in Zimbabwe? In other African countries and some parts of Asia, digital bookmobiles – usually vans that have been equipped with computers, printers, and a wireless Internet connection – have been making the rounds. Rural schoolchildren who've been visited by the Uganda Digital Bookmobile have been able to print and bind their own copies of dozens of copyright-free (or public domain) books, including the works of Beatrix Potter. In India, a digital bookmobile patrols dusty backroads, giving villagers and schoolchildren access to more than ten thousand books via the Internet. Each bus is also equipped with an e-mail server and a high-powered wireless base station, and can deliver and collect e-mail as it drives past. Eventually, the Indian government hopes to have these bookmobiles operating in each of the country's thirty districts.

As we saw in the previous chapter, some of the world's oldest libraries have also been turning to new technologies to give their users – and potential users – greater access to their collections. The British Library, for example, has digitized many

Bogotá's Biblored program provides free Internet service to an estimated 2.5 million Colombians.

The Dunhuang Documents

In 2002, the National Library of China and the British Library launched a website called the International Dunhuang Project (accessible in English at idp.bl.uk). This site makes available – to anyone, anywhere in the world – more than fifty thousand ancient manuscripts, paintings, and artifacts found along the Silk Road, a centuries-old trade route between China and Europe.

Visitors to the website can view digitized versions of original Silk Road documents. These include ancient prescriptions, a contract for the sale of a slave girl, and even a letter from a dinner guest apologizing for his drunken behavior. Taken together, they create an amazing portrait of day-to-day life along the Silk Road between the fifth and eleventh centuries.

The site is a great resource for professional historians and researchers, who can now view these rare documents without having to travel all the way to China to do so. But it's also there to be enjoyed by anyone who is simply interested in the history of China. This project is an exceptional example of how organizations that are separated by thousands of miles can nevertheless work together, using new technologies, to make valuable materials available to all those who want to see them.

priceless books and documents and made them available in an online gallery on its website. There, virtual visitors can compare two different editions of Gutenberg's Bible – books so rare and valuable that most scholars are not allowed to see or touch them. The website also features one of only four surviving copies of the Magna Carta, a thirteenth-century document that is considered by many to be the first constitution ever written.

The British Library has also launched an ambitious project known as the National Digital Library. In 2006, as part of this initiative, technologists will digitize about one hundred thousand

Digitization is the process by which data, like text and images, is converted into digital form. Digital files can be stored and viewed on any computer.

copyright-free books from the library's holdings. But this is only a drop in the ocean. The library has more than 150 million items in its collection, including books, manuscripts, patents, maps, and sound recordings. With today's technology, it takes a person about half an hour to scan a three-hundred-page book. If someone were to scan a hundred items a day, seven days a week, it would take about four thousand years to digitize the British Library's current collection. Of course, some of these books are so delicate and valuable that they're in danger of being damaged whenever they're touched by human hands. This is why some companies are working on producing automated scanners that will gently lift fragile pages with a puff of air and turn them using a light vacuum.

The National Digital Library is only one of many e-library initiatives currently in the works. The one that started it all, though, is Project Gutenberg (accessible at www.gutenberg.org). This online digital library currently has more than ten thousand

New automated book scanners have the potential to digitize more than a thousand pages of text an hour.

What Is the Public Domain?

In almost all countries, copyright law protects inventions and creative works like books and music (known as intellectual property) for the lifetime of the author plus a set number of years after his or her death (usually somewhere between twenty-five and seventy-five). These laws exist to safeguard intellectual property from unfair copying and to ensure that an author can earn money from his or her creation. When its copyright expires, a work is said to come into the public domain. From that point forward, anyone can make and sell copies of it without paying anything to the person who created the work in the first place.

Issues surrounding copyright law have become more complicated with the invention of the Internet. In 2000, the music industry successfully sued a file-sharing service called Napster for posting music files and allowing users to download them without paying royalties to the artists. And in 2005, a group of writers and book publishers filed a lawsuit against the search engine Google to halt its plans to scan and index millions of books, including ones still covered by copyright.

Throughout history, technological advances have often been met with distrust and even fear. Some feel that that's what's driving people's resistance to digital libraries and similar projects. But it's still important for content providers to find a way to balance the rights of authors, musicians, and filmmakers against the great promise held by the free exchange of ideas and information.

electronic books available in languages from English and French to Sanskrit and Welsh. All of the titles found on the Project Gutenberg website are in the public domain and can be downloaded for free in seconds. The site gets about two million downloads a month, and its collection includes authors like Sir Arthur Conan Doyle, the Brothers Grimm, Edgar Allan Poe, and Jane Austen. At the click of a mouse, users can acquire copies of Einstein's theory of relativity, the notebooks of Leonardo da Vinci, or some eighteenth-century lessons in the art of dancing – all entered, proofread, and checked and analyzed by volunteers.

Technology is transforming our libraries. It has been so influential, in fact, that some people wonder if they will eventually just cease to exist. While it's probably true that future libraries won't resemble the ones we use today, they will still have an important role to play. Libraries are treasures troves of

Ask a Librarian

Librarians are also called "information specialists" because they are so good at helping people find answers to their questions. They can find just about anything and will happily show even first-time visitors how to make sense of the most complicated information. Librarians must complete a lot of schooling – every one has an undergraduate university degree and a masters degree in library and information science. If you think you might like to become a librarian, visit www.becomealibrarian.org to find out more about what it's like. This American website includes stories from working librarians, information on degree programs, and a listing of volunteer and job-shadowing opportunities. But if you really want to know what working in a library is all about, just wander into your local branch and . . . ask a librarian!

ideas. They help us remember where we've been, and they provide us with the information and inspiration we need as we journey into the future. No matter what that future holds, they will continue to bring people and ideas together, just as they have always done.

NOTES

There are many good books about libraries, the history of writing and reading, and the development of culture. These notes acknowledge the ones I relied on most in writing this book. Also included here are references to websites that were of particular help and are not cited elsewhere in the book.

Chapter 1: In the Beginning
Some of the information about the scientists and scholars who used Alexandria's famous library, including Archimedes, came from *The Library of Alexandria* by Kelly Trumble (New York: Clarion, 2003). Some of the details of Hypatia's life come from the online version of the Encyclopaedia Britannica, accessible at www.britannica.com/eb/article-9041785. The information about what Aristotle's private library was like and how it was organized is drawn in part from *Libraries in the Ancient World* by Lionel Casson (New Haven, CN: Yale University Press, 2001). There are many websites that describe the villa of Lucius Piso and the efforts to read the recovered papyrus scrolls. See, especially, dsc.discovery.com/convergence/pompeii/history/excavations_04.html, the Discovery Channel's feature on Pompeii, and magazine.byu.edu/article.tpl?num=44-Spr01, a story about the work taking place at Brigham Young University to create a digital library of the charred scrolls. The Getty Museum in California also has a replica of Piso's villa; a video tour of the buildings is available online at www.humnet.ucla.edu/horaces-villa/study/HercVilla.html. Some of the

information about the public libraries of Rome is drawn from Casson's *Libraries in the Ancient World*.

Chapter 2: The Darkest Days
The story of the Muslim governor ordering the destruction of the scrolls of the Serapeum is drawn from *Library: An Unquiet History* by Matthew Battles (New York: Norton, 2003). The quote about all the closing libraries is noted in *A History of Libraries in the Western World* by Michael Harris (London: Scarecrow Press, 1995). A good description of the burning of Alexandria can be found in Trumble's *Library of Alexandria*. The quote about the laziness of the monks comes from *The Story of Libraries* by Fred Lerner (New York: Continuum, 1998). That book also provided many interesting details about life in the scriptoriums and about the hard work that went in to copying manuscripts, including the quote from the nameless monk. The anecdote about monks scratching themselves like dogs to signal that they needed a pagan book comes from *A History of Reading* by Alberto Manguel (Toronto: Vintage Canada, 1996). The quip about early librarians scratching out the names of unacceptable authors comes from Lerner's *Story of Libraries*. Numerous books refer to the grand vizier and his camel library, including Manguel's *History of Reading*. The story of the Mongols throwing all the books into the Tigris River comes from Harris's *History of Libraries in the Western World*.

Chapter 3: A Golden Age

Some of the details about Gutenberg and his printing press are drawn from *The A to Z of Everyday Things* by Janice Weaver (Toronto: Tundra Books, 2004). The information about the responsibilities of Renaissance librarians and the penalties for misuse of the books comes from Fred Lerner's *Story of Libraries*. That book also provided the quote from Petrarch, the one about the books calling out to be saved, and the one from Pope Leo X, justifying his theft of an important illuminated manuscript. Some of the information about the formation of the Bodleian Library is drawn from an article published in *Oxford Today*, the magazine of Oxford University, accessible at www.oxfordtoday.ox.ac.uk/2001-02/v14n2/03.shtml. The quotes from the Connecticut church leaders who founded Yale and from the president of Princeton University are both mentioned in *The Story of Libraries*.

Chapter 4: Into the New World

Some of the details about the life of Benjamin Franklin, and especially his interest in subscription libraries, are drawn from *Benjamin Franklin* by Edmund S. Morgan (New Haven, CN: Yale University Press, 2002). The quote about using libraries to promote virtuous habits is mentioned in Michael Harris's *History of Libraries in the Western World*. A good history of the Boston Public Library can be found on the library's website at www.bpl.org/guides/history.htm. Some of the information about Andrew Carnegie and his commitment to public libraries came from the book *Carnegie* by Peter Krass (Hoboken, NJ: Wiley, 2002). The quote about female librarians, made by the first president of the American Library Association, is cited in the paper "The History, Progression, and Issues of Women Librarians" by Annie L. Downey (accessible online at www.unt.edu/slis/students/projects/history_of_women_librarians.pdf). The website of the Prince Rupert [British Columbia] Public Library – accessible at www.bookboat.com – offers a great deal of information about unusual and mobile libraries, like the camel library in Kenya and the steamers of the Swedish archipelago.

Chapter 5: Back to the Future

The new library in Alexandria has an excellent website at www.bibalex.org/English/index.aspx. Visitors can view photos of the building, find out about upcoming events, and even buy Egyptian souvenirs. Some of the information about the Bill & Melinda Gates Foundation, and especially about the book boats of Bangladesh, is drawn from the foundation's website, accessible at www.gatesfoundation.org/default.htm. Statistical information about the Toronto Public Library was taken from the library's 2004 annual report. A few of the details about the library initiatives in Colombia came from "Biblored: Colombia's Innovative Library Network," a report by María Cristina Caballero. The report can be found on the website of the Council on Library and Information Resources at www.clir.org/. Information about the Uganda Digital Bookmobile came from an interview with Richard Koman, a driving force behind the project.

WHERE TO LOOK

Thanks to the Internet, you can check out all the great libraries of the world without even leaving home. Here's a sampling of some of the best sites on offer. Don't forget to look at your own local library's website too!

Bibliotheca Alexandrina
http://www.bibalex.org/English/index.aspx
The English version of the website for the new library in Alexandria offers links to online magazines and sites that specialize in Egyptian history.

Boston Public Library
http://www.bpl.org/
Enter the BPL's teen lounge for reading lists and links to dozens of cool music, movie, and TV sites. You can even get help with your homework!

British Library
http://www.bl.uk
In addition to its Turning the Pages exhibition and its online gallery of special treasures, the website for the British Library has areas where you can learn to make an ancient book or listen to a survivor's memories of the Holocaust.

Library and Archives Canada
http://www.collectionscanada.ca/
At the website for Canada's national library, you can explore the history of hockey, view newsreels from the Second World War, or learn how to create your own comic book.

Library of Congress
http://www.loc.gov/
This website features video- and audiotape interviews with former soldiers, as well as maps that date back to the 1500s. There's even a section that offers answers to everyday questions about plants, animals, technology, and science.

National Library of Australia
http://www.nla.gov.au
The National Treasures area of this website tells the story of Australia's colorful history using maps, manuscripts, drawings, paintings, and important artifacts.

National Library of France
http://www.bnf.fr/pages/version_anglaise/english.htm
The website for France's national library offers virtual exhibitions on a wide range of subjects — from the history of New France to the art of book binding in the Arabic world — in both English and French.

National Library of Québec
http://www.bnquebec.ca/portal/dt/accueil.html?bnq_langue=en
In the Digital Collections area of this site, web visitors can call up maps from the 1600s or browse through paintings by Quebec artists.

National Library of Singapore
http://www.nlb.gov.sg/
Singapore's World eBook Library has more than a

hundred thousand electronic books and documents ready for downloading.

New York Public Library
http://www.nypl.org/
In the TeenLink area of the New York Public Library site, you can read the work of young authors, get study tips, and download a list of recommended books.

Toronto Public Library
http://www.tpl.toronto.on.ca/
Log into the library's Ramp section to join a discussion group or submit your stories and poems to a writer in electronic residence. The site also lists local volunteer and job-shadowing opportunities for teens.

Salt Lake City Public Library
http://www.slcpl.lib.ut.us/index.jsp
Teens can download lists of chick lit favorites or books written by other young people. Visitors can also access links to websites recommended by library staff and an online calendar of local events.

Seattle Public Library
http://www.spl.org/
On the Seattle Public Library site, you can post your own book reviews or access lists of recommended books in a number of different genres, from horror to science fiction to fantasy.

Virtual Libraries

Many libraries exist solely in cyberspace and are accessible to visitors through the Internet. Virtual libraries make it possible for specialized information to be presented in innovative ways. Here are some great virtual libraries for you to take a look at.

African Digital Library
http://www.africandl.org.za

Google Library Project
http://print.google.com/googleprint/library.html

ibiblio
http://www.ibiblio.org/

Internet Archive
http://www.archive.org/

Internet Public Library
http://www.ipl.org/

National Science Digital Library
http://nsdl.org/

Project Gutenberg
http://www.gutenberg.org/

Library Associations

If you're looking for information about libraries and librarianship, professional associations are a great place to start. Whether you're interested in a career as a librarian or simply want to keep up with trends in information services, the websites listed below will help.

American Library Association
www.ala.org

Canadian Library Association
www.cla.ca

International Federation of Libraries Associations and Institutions (IFLA)
http://www.ifla.org/

ACKNOWLEDGMENTS

Libraries are my passion. My late mother, Rosemary Pitcher, was a newspaper reporter and travel writer who ensured that reading and regular trips to the library were always a part of my world. My decision to work in a public library is the direct result of our shared passion for the written word.

I'm very fortunate to have worked for two of the great public library systems in Canada. The librarians and staff of the Kitchener Public Library, where I began my career, and those at the Hamilton Public Library, where I work now, continue to inspire me every day. The Faculty of Information Studies at the University of Toronto, the Canadian Library Association, and the Northern Exposure to Leadership Program were all instrumental in helping me transform my passion into action.

I want to thank Kathy Lowinger for giving me the opportunity to work with Tundra again. What a gift this has been. I'm grateful to this book's designer, Kong Njo, for the wonderful work he has done with the layout. And the illustrations by the incomparable Bill Slavin are truly spectacular.

Finally, I thank my editor, Janice Weaver. Without her perceptive comments, challenging questions, and expert attention, this book would not have been possible. Thank you, Janice.

INDEX